Every animal likes freedom.

Singing birds make us happy.

A monkey in silk is no less a monkey.

I will feed my cat

English Grammar

Workbook 2

Dogs are my favourite animal.

Rhino _ _ ros

Om KIDZ
An imprint of Om Books International

SENTENCE SCRAMBLE

Happy the Hippo has messed up his sentences! Tick the ones that make sense and cross out the ones that don't.

Cuckoos sweet sing.

Mary has a little lamb.

I going to are the zoo.

I will feed my cat.

My animal favourite are dog.

Camels are usually found in deserts.

Is the monkey eating a banana?

NAME SORTING

Help Tickles the Tiger sort out the nouns from these sentences in the correct column.

A herd of cattle is passing by.

Mojo the monkey is looking at me.

Elephants are the largest animals on land.

We named our dog Lucy.

The Gir forest has lions.

Have you seen that litter of kittens?

The hyena's laughter was scary.

Proper	Common	Abstract	Collective

ONCE UPON A NOUN

Help Bingo the Bear underline the countable nouns in **BLUE** and the uncountable nouns in **RED**.

Once upon a time, there lived a family of three bears in the woods. They were Mama Bear, Papa Bear and Baby Bear. One day, they went out for a walk. Mama Bear cooked up some delicious porridge before they left.

While they were gone, a little girl named Goldilocks walked by their house. She smelt the porridge and her tummy began to rumble. She went in and saw three bowls on the table.

She ran towards them and took a spoonful of Papa Bear's porridge. But it was too hot. Then, she grabbed a spoonful of Mama Bear's porridge. But it was too cold. Finally, she tried Baby Bear's porridge. It was just right! She ate it all up hungrily.

After a while, she felt sleepy. She spotted Papa Bear's bed, but it was too hard. She lay down on Mama Bear's bed, but it was too soft. Finally, she tried Baby Bear's bed, which was just right. She jumped onto the bed and fell asleep in a jiffy!

Soon, the bears returned home. Baby Bear started crying when he saw his porridge bowl empty. "Somebody ate all my porridge!" he cried and ran to his room. And what did he see there? A strange little girl fast asleep on his bed! Baby bear screamed loudly. Goldilocks woke up. She was shocked to see three angry bears at the foot of the bed. She jumped out and ran away as fast as she could.

SENTENCE SORTER

Let's help Laurie the Lion circle the subjects and underline the predicates in the sentences below.

Singing birds make us happy.

A camel is called the ship of the desert.

Forests have a variety of trees.

Cows give us milk.

Wild animals live in jungles.

Dogs are a man's best friend.

SOUND ALIKE

Help Hagrid the Hippo choose the correct homophones to complete the sentence.

A horse is ______, whereas a mare is female.

a. mail b. male

There are ______ many bees in this forest.

a. too b. two

We saw a ______ on our hiking trip.

a. deer b. dear

Did you ______ the sound of the bear?

a. here b. hear

The cat is ______ favourite pet.

a. their b. there

The ______ lost the race.

a. hair b. hare

ARTICLE TRACKER

Leo the Leopard wrote a poem but forgot to add articles.
Can you add articles in the correct places?

Once there was ________ cute little leopard.
But he didn't want to be cute.
He wanted to be __________ shepherd!

What he loved most was to keep
__________ close, watchful eye
on those naughty little sheep.

He liked to watch them graze all day.
Then lead them back home
for __________ good night's stay.

But the sheep didn't like
__________ leopard too much.
They were afraid of his sharp touch.

When they saw __________ leopard coming by
they ran as fast
as their little feet could try.

__________ leopard was sad, but what could he do.
He gave up being __________ shepherd
and went to __________ zoo!

VERBIE WORM

Verbie the Worm wants you to circle all the verbs in these sentences and connect them to his basket.

The hungry lion is roaring.

The owl is hiding because it is daytime.

The crow is flying down to steal the cheese.

Goldilocks fell asleep on baby bear's bed.

The animals are drinking water from the stream.

Why is your dog walking like that?

She took her cat to the vet.

All his friends thanked the bear.

The crafty fox hides behind that bush every day.

A tiny mouse lived in the hole.

TIGER TENSE

Help Timmy the Tiger name the tenses of the underlined words. Write whether they are present, past or future tense on the blanks below.

The bird is flying high up in the sky.

____

I will take my dog for a walk shortly.

____

The boy saw how the elephant was being bathed.

____

The cat rolled in the sand and got dirty.

____

My pet dog is drinking milk this morning.

____

ADJECTIVE HUNT

Ronnie the Rhino is on an adjective quest. Spot and circle all the adjectives in the grid.

s	l	e	b	s	l	e	p	o	n	g
w	q	f	e	r	o	c	t	g	r	u
i	w	b	a	i	w	k	m	r	u	m
m	f	e	r	o	c	i	o	u	s	p
g	r	a	c	e	f	u	l	m	c	g
i	w	u	i	i	w	k	m	p	a	m
m	e	t	p	r	e	t	t	y	r	p
m	h	i	u	m	s	l	i	m	y	g
i	w	f	l	d	h	i	l	a	z	y
n	z	u	n	n	y	k	n	z	a	n
s	h	l	g	g	p	u	w	i	l	d

QUALITY OR QUANTITY?

Read the sentences and help Jenny the Giraffe decide whether they have adjectives of quality or quantity.

The dog has two puppies. ______________

The giraffe is a tall animal. ______________

The crafty fox wanted the cheese. ______________

Some birds cannot fly. ______________

There are many species of animals, birds and insects to be found. ______________

Elephants have long trunks. ______________

Dinosaurs are extinct animals. ______________

ARNIE'S ADVERBS

Arnie the Ant wants to fill up the jungle with adverbs. Help him add the correct ones to these sentences first!

Hyenas laugh ______________.

A cat can catch a mouse ______________.

Cheetahs run ______________.

We ______________ go trekking in the forest.

The little bird sang ______________.

GENDER BENDER

Builder Beaver is constructing a gender chart. Can you help him fill in the correct words?

If a cow is female, a male is a __________.

If a tigress is female, a male is a __________.

If a lioness is female, a male is a __________.

If a sow is a female panda, a male is a __________.

If a hen is female, a male is a __________.

COUNT AND MATCH

Match these singular animals to their plural forms.

macaw	squirrels
squirrel	rhinoceroses
rhinoceros	mongooses
mongoose	macaws

WORD WHIZ

Help Oliver the Owl understand synonyms and antonyms. Read the sentences. Mark the synonyms with 'S' and the antonyms with 'A' in the boxes alongside.

This is a dense forest.	crammed		clear	
Wild beasts inhabit the forest.	tamed		untamed	
Pretty flowers grow amidst the trees.	beautiful		ugly	
Our ecology needs to be preserved.	destroyed		conserved	
The berries that grow here are delicious.	nasty		tasty	
A clear stream is flowing here.	murky		clean	
The antelope has big horns.	small		large	

PICKING PRONOUNS

Pinto the Parrot needs to pick out the correct pronouns to complete these sentences. Can you help him?

(I / She) like animals.

Jack and (I / me) are watching a movie about bears.

(That / These) puppy needs water.

Dolly likes turtles. (She / He) has got one as a pet.

Mary told (me / I) an interesting story about elephants.

LEAFY LINKS

Choose the correct word from the flowers to complete the sentences below.

There are clouds ______ the sky.

The sun is shining from ______ the clouds.

The giraffe is walking ______ the elephant.

Can you see that bird ______ the two trees?

The crocodile is swimming ______ the river.

We can see fish swimming ______ the water.

The woodpecker vanished ______ its nest.

Flowers are growing ______ those trees.

The monkey is swinging ______ tree to tree.

The shepherd is sitting ______ his sheep.

in from behind near

under beside between across

COME TOGETHER

Join and rewrite the following sentences using a preposition from the flowers.

as | so | even | because
though | since | when | while

The fox wanted the cheese. He flattered the crow.

____

The turtle didn't give up. He was slow.

____

No one came to help the shepherd. He had cried wolf many times.

____

____

The ant did not help the grasshopper. He was lazy.

____

The stork ate her dinner. The fox watched.

____

ERROR SPOTTER

Spot and circle the errors in the sentences below.

Where I can find a pet shop?

We have visited Ranthambore sanctuary last weekend.

The woman which works as forest officer is from my city.

Although it was raining but we had the hike.

I look forward to meet my friends outside the woods.

Every animals likes freedom.

EXCLAIM THAT!

Spot and circle the interjections from the pebbles below.

Ouch

Water

Phew

Book

Hey

Yikes

Oh no

Grammar

Wow

Coffee

Turtle

Soup

PROVERB PROBLEMS

Mojo the Monkey messed up all these proverbs! Rearrange the words in the correct order to make meaningful proverbs.

change leopard spots cannot A its

silk monkey monkey less no A is a in

rotten barrel A spoils apple the

An snared old easily fox not is

paints A picture words thousand a

The worm the early catches bird

can lead can't a drink horse to,
you make You but water him

INSPECTOR IDIOM

Help Inspector Eagle spot and circle the idioms in these sentences.

Please be clear, do not beat around the bush.

Trying to learn karate like this is not right, you are barking up the wrong tree.

Let someone else hear that cock and bull story.

Cry wolf, and you are sure to learn your lesson.

The first ranker turned out to be a dark horse.

Don't count your chickens before they hatch.

Hold your horses, hard work always pays.

SPELLCHECK

Help these animals spell their names correctly by filling the blanks with the correct letters.

Rhino _ _ ros

Hippopo _ _ mus

T _ _ can

M _ _ aw

R _ _ ndeer

PUNCTUATION PROBLEMS

Help Rory the Reindeer rewrite these sentences with the correct punctuation marks.

where is the dogs kennel

jills dog is barking

Wow I like your goldfish.

I saw elephants giraffes zebras and bears at the zoo

oh I love this book about different forests

ALL ABOUT ANIMALS

Read the paragraph below and answer the questions on the next page.

The jungle stretches over vast expanses. For miles and miles, all you see is a stretch of land. Wait! A quick streak seems to be moving through this wide, empty space. If you look closely, you can see a spotted blur running at an unbelievable speed. It is the cheetah, the fastest animal on land.

Cheetahs have long, slender bodies that help them move at a quick pace. They use their tails to steer in the right direction.

These amazing animals belong to the cat family, just like lions and tigers. However, unlike their cousins, cheetahs do not let out loud, scary roars. They purr, just like your friendly little house cat!

Cheetahs hunt mostly during the day, either late in the morning or early in the evening. They chase their prey and pounce on them in a matter of seconds, gobbling up their meals instantly.

Who is the fastest animal on land?

___

Which family does the cheetah belong to?

___

What sound does a cheetah make?

___

When do cheetahs hunt?

___

How do cheetahs move in different directions while running?

___

DEAR ANIMALS

Bobby wants to write a letter to all the animals he visited when he went to the jungle. Can you help him write the letter?

To,

From,

FABULOUS FABLES

Look at the picture, read the lines below and complete the rest of the story.

Once upon a time, there lived a lazy shepherd boy. He didn't look after his sheep too well. Everyday, he took his sheep up the hill and left them alone while he napped under a tree. One day, ______________________________

JUNGLE QUEST

Let's write a story about the jungle. Look at these animals and write a story about them.

ANSWERS

Page 2

Cuckoos sweet sing.	✗
Mary has a little lamb.	✓
I going to are the zoo.	✗
I will feed my cat.	✓
My animal favourite are dog.	✗
Camels are usually found in deserts.	✓
Is the monkey eating a banana?	✓

Page 3

Proper	Common	Abstract	Collective
Mojo	cattle	laughter	herd
Lucy	monkey		litter
Gir	elephants		
	lions		
	animals		
	dog		
	forest		
	kittens		
	hyena		

Pages 4-5

Once upon a time, there lived a family of three bears in the woods. They were Mama Bear, Papa Bear and Baby Bear. One day, they went out for a walk. Mama Bear cooked up some delicious porridge before they left.

While they were gone, a little girl named Goldilocks walked by their house. She smelt the porridge and her tummy began to rumble. She went in and saw three bowls on the table. She ran towards them and took a spoonful of Papa Bear's porridge. But it was too hot. Then, she grabbed a spoonful of Mama Bear's porridge. But it was too cold. Finally, she tried Baby Bear's porridge. It was just right! She ate it all up hungrily.

After a while, she felt sleepy. She spotted Papa Bear's bed, but it was too hard.

She lay down on Mama Bear's bed, but it was too soft. Finally, she tried Baby Bear's bed, which was just right. She jumped onto the bed and fell asleep in a jiffy!

Soon, the bears returned home. Baby Bear started crying when he saw his porridge bowl empty. "Somebody ate all my porridge!" he cried and ran to his room. And what did he see there? A strange little girl fast asleep on his bed! Baby bear screamed loudly. Goldilocks woke up. She was shocked to see three angry bears at the foot of the bed. She jumped out and ran away as fast as she could.

Page 6

Singing birds make us happy.

A camel is called the ship of the desert.

Forests have a variety of trees.

Cows give us milk.

Wild animals live in jungles.

Dogs are a man's best friend.

Page 7

A horse is the male , whereas the mare is the female.

There are too many bees in this forest.

We saw a deer on our hiking trip.

Did you hear the sound of the bear?

The cat is their favourite pet.

The hare lost the race.

Page 8

Once there was **a** cute little leopard.
But he didn't want to be cute.
He wanted to be **a** shepherd!

What he loved most was to keep
a close, watchful eye
on those naughty little sheep.

He liked to watch them graze all day.
Then lead them back home
for **a** good night's stay.

But the sheep didn't like **the** leopard too much.
They were afraid of his sharp touch.

When they saw **the** leopard coming by
they ran as fast
as their little feet could try.

The leopard was sad, but what could he do.
He gave up being **a** shepherd
and went to **a** zoo!

Page 9

The hungry lion is roaring.

The owl is hiding because it is daytime.

The crow is flying down to steal the cheese.

Goldilocks fell asleep on baby bear's bed.

The animals are drinking water from the stream.

Why is your dog walking like that?

She took her cat to the vet.

All his friends thanked the bear.

The crafty fox hides behind that bush every day.

A tiny mouse lived in the hole.

Page 10

The bird is flying high up in the sky.
present tense

I will take my dog for a walk shortly.
future tense

The boy saw how the elephant was being bathed.
past tense

The cat rolled in the sand and got dirty.
past tense

My pet dog is drinking milk this morning.
present tense

Page 11

s	l	e	b	s	l	e	p	o	n	g
w	q	f	e	r	o	c	t	g	r	u
i	w	b	a	i	w	k	m	r	u	m
m	f	e	r	o	c	i	o	u	s	p
g	r	a	c	e	f	u	l	m	c	g
i	w	u	i	i	w	k	m	p	a	m
m	e	t	p	r	e	t	t	y	r	p
m	h	i	u	m	s	l	i	m	y	g
i	w	f	l	d	h	i	l	a	z	y
n	z	u	n	n	y	k	n	z	a	n
s	h	l	g	g	p	u	w	i	l	d

Page 12

The dog has two puppies.
adjective of quantity

The giraffe is a tall animal.
adjective of quality

The crafty fox wanted the cheese.
adjective of quality

Some birds cannot fly.
adjective of quantity

There are many species of animals, birds and insects to be found.
adjective of quantity

Elephants have long trunks.
adjective of quality

Dinosaurs are extinct animals.
adjective of quality

Page 13

Hyenas laugh **loudly**.

A cat can catch a mouse **easily**.

Cheetahs run **quickly**.

We **often** go trekking in the forest.

The little bird sang **joyfully**.

Page 14

If a cow is female, a male is a **bull**.

If a tigress is female, a male is a **tiger**.

If a lioness is female, a male is a **lion**.

If a sow is a female panda, a male is a **bear**.

If a hen is female, a male is a **rooster**.

Page 15

macaw	macaws
squirrel	squirrels
rhinoceros	rhinoceroses
mongoose	mongooses

Page 16

This is a dense forest.

Wild beasts inhabit the forest.

Pretty flowers grow amidst the trees.

Our ecology needs to be preserved.

The berries that grow here are delicious.

A clear stream is flowing here.

The antelope has big horns.

crammed	S	clear	A
tamed	A	untamed	S
beautiful	S	ugly	A
destroyed	A	conserved	S
nasty	A	tasty	S
murky	A	clean	S
small	A	large	S

Page 17

(**I** / She) like animals.

Jack and (**I** / me) are watching a movie about bears.

(**That** / These) puppy needs water.

Dolly likes turtles. (**She** / He) has got one as a pet.

Mary told (**me** / I) an interesting story about elephants.

ANSWERS

Page 18

There are clouds **in** the sky.

The sun is shining from **behind** the clouds.

The giraffe is walking **beside** the elephant.

Can you see that bird **between** the two trees?

The crocodile is swimming **across** the river.

We can see fish swimming **under** the water.

The woodpecker vanished **near** its nest.

Flowers are growing **near** those trees.

The monkey is swinging **from** tree to tree.

The shepherd is sitting **near** his sheep.

Page 19

The fox wanted the cheese. He flattered the crow.
The fox wanted the cheese **so** he flattered the crow.

The turtle didn't give up. He was slow.
The turtle didn't give up **even though** he was slow.

No one came to help the shepherd. He had cried wolf many times.
No one came to help the shepherd **because** he had cried wolf many times.

The ant did not help the grasshopper. He was lazy.
The ant did not help the grasshopper **because** he was lazy.

The stork ate her dinner. The fox watched.
The stork ate her dinner **while** the fox watched.

Page 20

Where I can find a pet shop?

We have visited Ranthambore sanctuary last weekend.

The woman which works as forest officer is from Maharashtra.

Although it was raining but we had the hike.

I look forward to meet my friends outside the woods.

Every animals likes freedom.

Page 21

Page 22

change leopard spots cannot A its
A leopard cannot change its spots.

silk monkey monkey less no A is a in
A monkey in silk is no less a monkey.

rotten barrel A spoils apple the
A rotten apple spoils the barrel.

An snared old easily fox not is
An old fox is not easily snared.

paints A picture words thousand a
A picture paints a thousand words.

The worm the early catches bird
The early bird catches the worm.

can lead can't a drink horse to, you make You but water him
You can lead a horse to water but you can't make him drink.

Page 23

Please be clear, do not beat around the bush.

Trying to learn karate like this is not right, you are barking up the wrong tree.

Let someone else her that cock and bull story.

Cry wolf and you are sure to learn your lesson.

The first ranker turned out to be a dark horse.

Don't count your chickens before they hatch.

Hold your horses, hard work always pays.

Page 24

Page 25

where is the dogs kennel
Where is the dog's kennel?

jills dog is barking
Jill's dog is barking.

Wow I like your goldfish.
Wow! I like your goldfish.

I saw elephants giraffes zebras and bears at the zoo
I saw elephants, giraffes, zebras and bears at the zoo.

oh I love this book about different forests
Oh! I love this book about different forests.

Pages 26-27

Answer the questions given below.

Who is the fastest animal on land?
The cheetah.

Which family does the cheetah belong to?
The cat family.

What sound does a cheetah make?
A purring sound.

When do cheetahs hunt?
Mostly during the day, either late in the morning or early in the evening.

How do cheetahs move in different directions while running?
They use their tails to steer in the right direction.